A COLLECTION OF
ANIMAL TALES

p

This is a Parragon Publishing book
This edition published in 2003
Parragon Publishing, Queen Street House,
4 Queen Street, Bath BA1 1HE, UK

Copyright © Parragon 2002

Puppy's Paw and Bouncy Bunny
Illustrated by Julie Nicholson.
Kissable Kitten illustrated by Julie Nicholson and
Andrew Everitt-Stewart.
Puppy's Paw and Bouncy Bunny written by Kay Barnes.
Kissable Kitten written by Jackie Andrews.

ISBN 0-75259-845-7

Printed in China

CONTENTS

This book belongs to...

....

BOUNCY
BUNNY

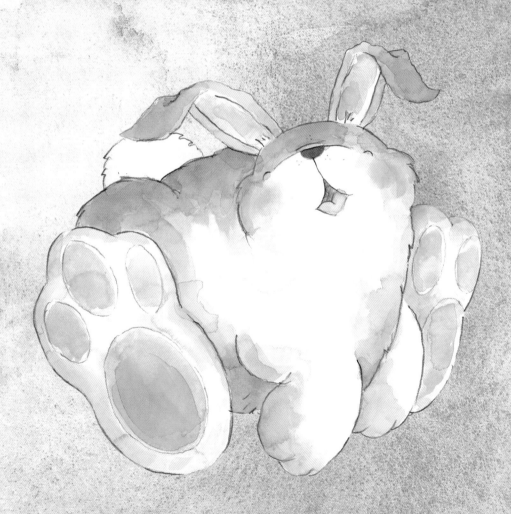

Mommy Rabbit had four beautiful babies. Three of them were tiny, soft balls of fluff— they were cuddly, quiet, and very, very cute. They never made a noise and always did exactly what their mommy told them.

And then there was Benny!

Benny wasn't like his brother and
sisters at all. He was large and loud and he
had the biggest bunny feet in the whole world.

And he loved to bounce! From dawn to dusk,
Benny bounced everywhere—

THUMP! THUMP! THUMP!

Benny never did what Mommy Rabbit told him, but she loved him just the same.

Early one morning, Mommy Rabbit was
woken by a very loud noise that made the
whole burrow wibble and wobble.
Soon, everyone was wide awake.
What was that noise?

It was Benny, of course,
bouncing and boinging around the
burrow on his big, flat feet!

"I'm *sure* he doesn't mean to be so
noisy," said Mommy Rabbit, with a
big yawn.

Benny bounced outside. Mommy Rabbit
followed him, twitching her nose and
checking for danger — *where had he
disappeared to?*

Suddenly, there was a loud —
THUMP! **THUMP! THUMP!**

"I'm hungry," said Benny, bouncing past her.
"I want my breakfast now, Mommy!"

By the time all the bunnies had come out of the burrow and into the sunshine, Benny had bounced round the meadow three times!

14

"Benny, stop jumping around!"
said Mommy Rabbit.
"Stay with the others.
It's dangerous out here."

"Now then, children," whispered Mommy Rabbit. "We're going over to the carrot field for breakfast. You must all stay very close to me and don't wander from the path."

But, of course, Benny didn't listen. With one huge **bounce,** he disappeared through a hole in the hedge and was gone!

"Oh, dear! Oh, dear! Oh, dear!" said his mother. "What is he up to now?"

"Benny Bunny!" said Mommy
Rabbit. "Where did you get
that lettuce?"

18

"In that field!" replied Benny.

"You might have been caught," said Mommy.

"I'm much too fast!" said Benny.

"Hurry, children," said Mommy Rabbit. "We must get to the carrot field before the farmer starts work."

But, of course, Benny wasn't listening. He was nibbling a dandelion.

"Hmm, tasty!" he mumbled to himself.

"Benny Bunny!" called
Mommy Rabbit. "Stop that munching and
follow me!"

Mommy Rabbit hopped under the gate and into the field. She collected lots of crunchy carrots.

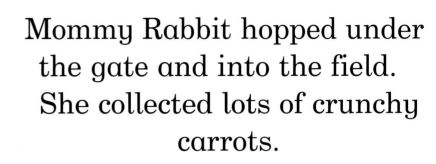

"Remember," she warned her bunnies. "Eat as much as you can but stay close to me and watch out for the farmer."

The carrots were wonderful—
fat and juicy, and crisp.
Soon, Benny's brother
and sisters were all
chewing happily.

Benny bounced
around on his big,
flat feet, nibbling,
and munching
as he went.
**Boing!
Boing!
Boing!**

Mommy Rabbit and her bunnies munched their way across the field, nibbling a leaf here, crunching a carrot there. No one noticed that little Tufty, Benny's baby brother, wasn't following them.

Suddenly, Mommy Rabbit heard the **roar** of the tractor.

"Quick!" she cried. "The farmer's coming!"

Everyone hopped into the hedge — except for Tufty!

Mommy Rabbit saw the tractor
heading straight for Tufty.
Its big wheels were churning
up the ground, squashing
everything in its path.

Her little baby crouched
by the fence, his paws over
his eyes, too terrified to move.

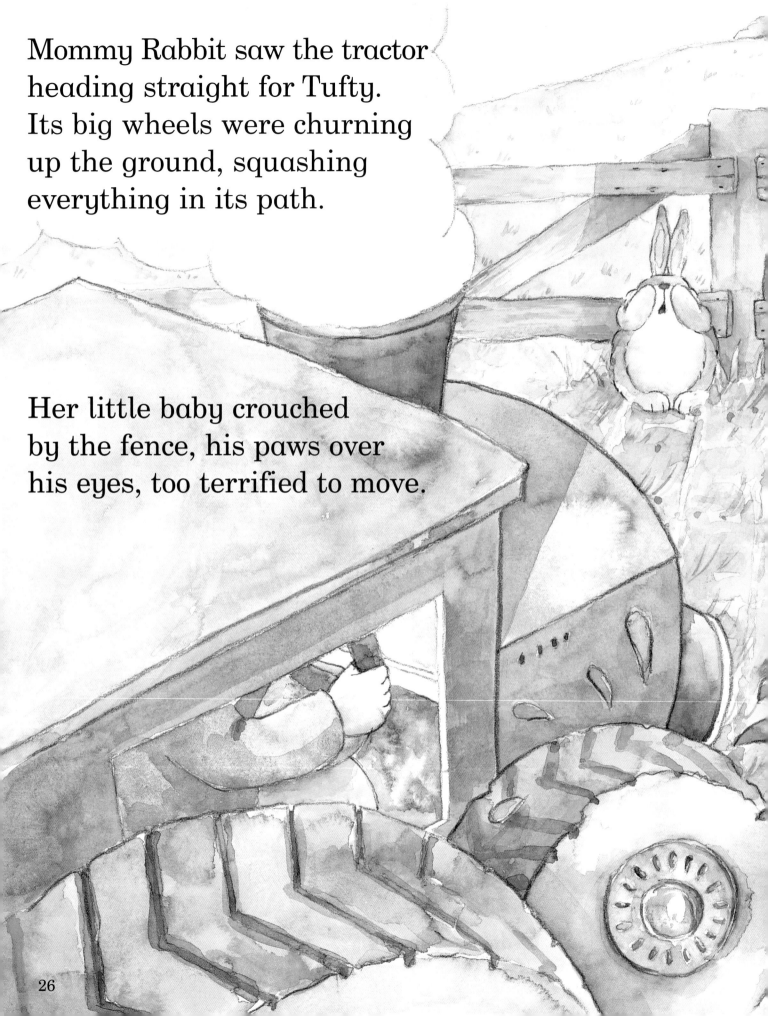

What could Mommy Rabbit do?

Suddenly, in a flash,
Benny Bunny bounced past!

In one huge bound,
Benny was by Tufty's side.
He bounced his brother
out of the way, just before
the tractor ran over him!

28

"I told you I was fast," giggled Benny.

"Benny Bunny!" said Mommy Rabbit, hopping over to Tufty and Benny. "You're so… "

"I know! I know!" said Benny. "I'm so *bouncy!*"

"Oh, no!" said Mommy Rabbit.
"I'm so glad that you *are* such a
bouncy bunny!"
and she gave him a great big kiss.

31

The End

PUPPY'S
PAW

One sunny day, a small puppy sat in a grassy yard, watching Snowball and Snowdrop, his brother and sister, play. His coat was white with a few brown patches — and he had one brown paw.

When he was born, his mommy said, "He looks like he's forgotten to put his other socks on!"

And that is how Socks got his name.

Socks asked his brother and sister if he could
play with them. "Can I join in?" yapped Socks.
"No, you can't!" Snowball barked back.

"He looks like he's been having a mud bath, with those brown splodges," sneered Snowdrop. "Go and wash yourself properly, Socks."

"Maybe we should wash him," laughed Snowball. And the two puppies chased Socks towards the bird bath.

Socks ran off as fast as he could and
hid inside the shed—why didn't
they like him? Was it because he
didn't look like them?

A big tear fell from his eye and
trickled down his nose.

Then, the two bouncy
puppies appeared.

"Socks, where are you?"
barked Snowdrop.

Socks peeped out from
his hiding place.

"We're going to the wood for a walk, Socks,"
called Snowball. "Bye-bye!"

Socks couldn't help himself. He ran out from
behind the shed. "Please can I come?" he begged.

"You're much too
young to come
with us," said
Snowdrop. "And you know
Mommy says that you're too young
to go out without her."

"I'm not too young," whined Socks.
"I've been out loads of times."

"Well, you can't walk with us," said Snowball. "You must walk behind us."

"Okay," yapped Socks, eagerly.

So, the two pups scampered through the yard gate, with Socks following.

Snowball and Snowdrop ran down the lane
towards the wood — Socks trotted behind!

In a clearing,
there were two paths to
choose from. Snowball's nose
began to twitch. He could smell
something wonderful.

"This way!" he yelped and the two
older pups rushed off.

"Don't those two ever stop
to look where they're
going?" wondered Socks,
as he lifted his brown
paw and followed.

Round a bend, the puppies found a huge clump of beautiful, pink flowers. Socks pushed his soft, black nose into them.

"Atishoo!" he sneezed, as yellow pollen flew into the air.

Snowdrop was busy chasing a butterfly. It fluttered away down another path and Snowdrop followed.

"Come on, Socks!" barked Snowball. "Keep up!" and he set off after his sister.

"We'll get lost if we're not careful," thought Socks.

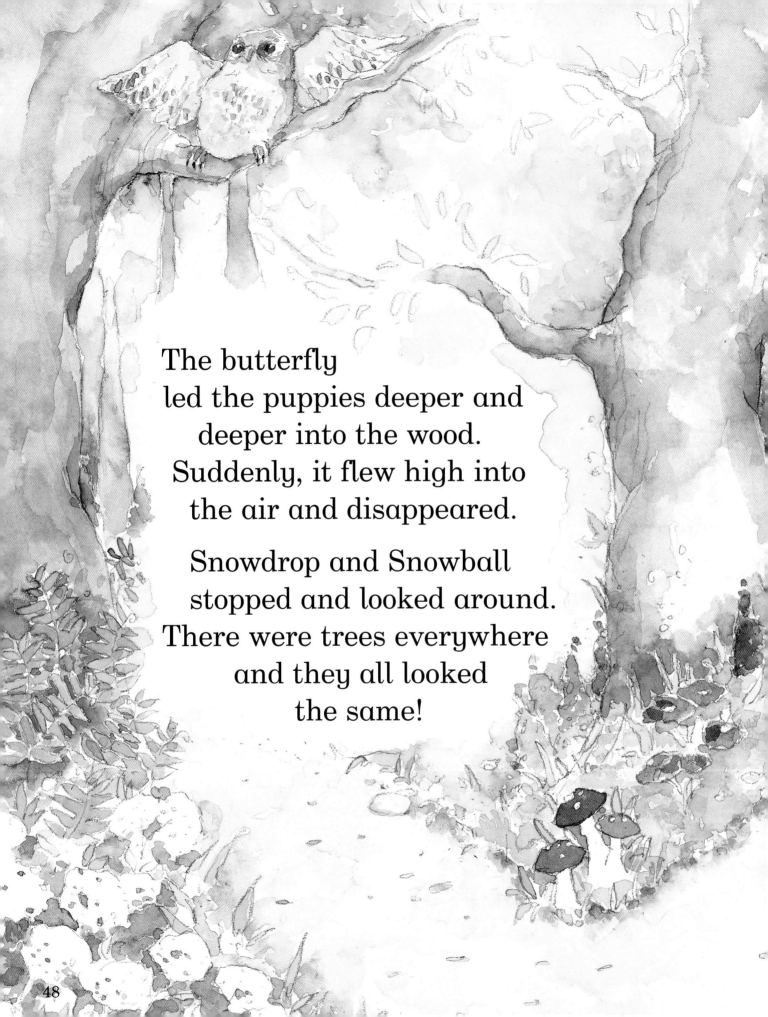

The butterfly
led the puppies deeper and
deeper into the wood.
Suddenly, it flew high into
the air and disappeared.

Snowdrop and Snowball
stopped and looked around.
There were trees everywhere
and they all looked
the same!

"How are we going to
find our way home now?"
wailed Snowball.

"Listen," woofed Snowdrop.
"There's someone through those
trees. Let's see if they know the way
home."

"I know the way… "
began Socks.

But Snowball and
Snowdrop weren't
listening. They had
already dashed off along
the path.

"It's easy," thought Socks to
himself, and set off after the others.

Tap-tap! Tap-tap!

A woodpecker was trying to find some insects in a tree.

"Can you help us find our way home?" asked Snowball and Snowdrop.

But the woodpecker flew off!

"What are we going to do now?"
whined Snowdrop. "I want my mommy!"

"Help!" they howled. "Help!"

"But *I* know the way home!" said Socks.

Snowdrop and Snowball turned to their brother
and stared. "What did you say?" they asked.

"I said I know the way home," said Socks, again.

"How?" asked Snowball.

"It's easy," said Socks. "Every time we chose a path, we took the one on the side of my brown paw. To get home, we just turn round and take the path on the side of my white paw. Follow me and I'll show you."

So, back through the woods they
went, with Socks in front.
Each time they had to
choose, Socks held up
his brown paw…

… turned his head and
took the other path.

Back they scampered
through the wood,
past the pink flowers…`

… down the lane…

… through the gate and into the yard,
where their mommy was waiting for them.

"Where have you been?"
she woofed, angrily.
"I've been so
worried."

"We got lost," said Snowball and Snowdrop.
"It was all our fault."

"Socks was so smart," woofed Snowball.
"We're so lucky to have him as a brother."

"I wish I had a brown paw like him," said Snowdrop. "Do you want to play ball, Socks?"

"Oh, yes please!" he yapped, flicking the ball across the grass to his brother and sister. Sometimes it was good to be different!

The End

KISSABLE
KITTEN

In a corner of the kitchen, Mommy Cat lay in her basket and purred happily. Curled up asleep beside her, were four beautiful kittens— a gray kitten called Timmy, a black kitten called Winnie, and a stripy kitten called Ginger.

And then there was Kissy, the softest, cutest kitten you ever did see!

Timmy had the biggest blue eyes.
They spotted everything.

When he and Kissy
were in the yard,
chasing bumble bees,
it was Timmy who spied
the water sprinkler.

"Watch out, Kissy!" said Timmy, "you'll get wet!"

"Splish, splash, flipperty-flash!" sang Kissy. "I don't care!"

Kissy pushed through the flowers with her little pink nose and shrieked with laughter, as the water sprinkler suddenly covered them both with water.

"Kissy!" spluttered Timmy, shaking water drops from his ears. "Now look what you've done!"

But Kissy just rolled around, laughing. "Oh, Timmy," she giggled. "That was *so* funny!"

"Goodness me," said Mommy Cat, as her kittens dripped water onto the kitchen floor. "Timmy Kitten! You shouldn't have let Kissy get so wet! Now I shall have to dry you both!"

Kissy wriggled and giggled,
as Mommy Cat's rough,
pink tongue made her
wet fur soft and white again.

"Sugar and spice, that feels nice!"

she sang.

But Timmy wasn't
quite so happy.
"Ow! Miaow!"
he howled, as
Mommy Cat's
tongue licked
him dry.

Kissy loved to explore
with Winnie.

Winnie had
the cutest kitten
nose ever and
could sniff out
all the best
yummy food.

"Mmm! Smells like jelly and cream,"
said Winnie, her nose and
whiskers twitching.

Kissy reached up and gently pulled a corner of the tablecloth.

"Careful, Kissy!" said Winnie. "You'll pull everything over!"

"Yum, yum, yum, that cream should be in my tum!"

sang Kissy.

Kissy pulled the cloth a bit more. Suddenly, the cream jug and jelly pot fell to the floor with a crash!

"Oh, Kissy!" shrieked Winnie.
  "What have you done?"

Jelly and cream went everywhere—
what a mess! Kissy Kitten could hardly
speak for laughing.

"Oh, Winnie," she giggled. "That was *so* funny!"

Mommy Cat threw her paws in the air,
when she saw the mess. "Goodness me," she said.
"How could you let Kissy get so sticky, Winnie Kitten?
Now I shall have to wash you both!"

Kissy giggled, as Mommy Cat licked her clean.

"Bibble and bat, I like that!"

she sang.

But Winnie wasn't happy at all.
"Ow! Miaow!" she cried, as Mommy Cat's
tongue lapped up the jelly.

Kissy loved playing with Ginger because Ginger liked to pretend he was a fierce tiger, hunting wild animals or pouncing on Mommy Cat's twitching tail.

Today, they were both hunting a monster mouse in the vegetable patch.

"There's a dangerous mud puddle over there, Kissy," whispered Ginger. "Whatever you do, *don't* go in it!"

"Fiddle, fuddle, who cares for a puddle?" sang Kissy.

Kissy crawled right through the sticky, squelchy mud.

Her beautiful white coat got muddier and muddier. She looked as if she was wearing brown boots!

Ginger hid his eyes. "I can't look!" he said.

Kissy laughed and laughed.
Then, she shook the mud off her dainty paws—
all over Ginger!

Mommy Cat howled when she
saw her two dirty kittens.

"Ginger Kitten! How could you have let
Kissy get so muddy?" she cried.
"It will take me ages to clean you both!"

Kissy wriggled, as Mommy Cat licked her clean.

"Piddle and pud, that feels good!"

she sang.

Poor Ginger didn't feel good at all. "Ow! Miaow!" he wailed, as Mommy Cat cleaned up his coat.

Mommy Cat looked at her kittens and shook her head. "I just can't understand it," she said. "You've always been such *good* kittens!"

Timmy, Winnie, and Ginger all frowned at Kissy, who was fast asleep, purring in their basket.
"It wasn't us!" they cried.

"We *told* Kissy Kitten to be careful!
We don't like being bathed!" cried the kittens.

"We don't like getting soaked...

or covered with sticky stuff...

or coated with mud!"

Mommy Cat looked into the basket.
"Kissy?" she said.

Kissy opened a bright, green eye and said,
"But Mommy, I just *love* it when you kiss my nose
and wash me every time I get messy!"

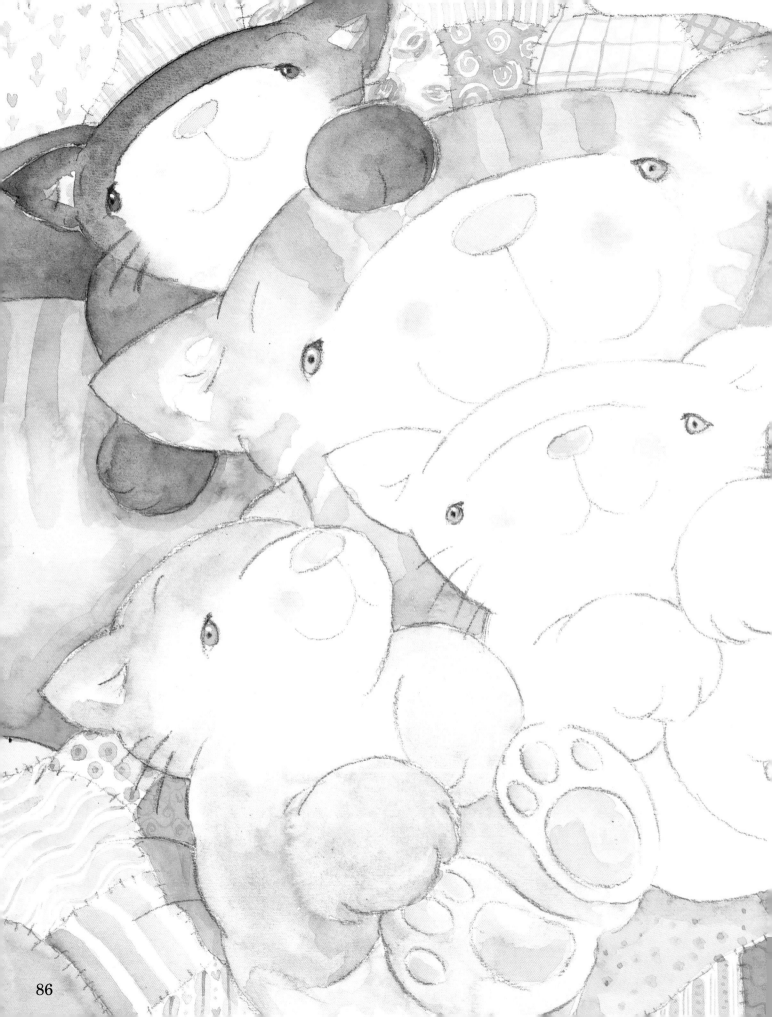

"What a funny Kissy
Kitten you are!"
said Mommy Cat,
giving her a big
lick. "You can have
a kiss any time
you want. You don't
have to get really
messy first!"

"No, we'd prefer it if
you didn't!" said Timmy.

"But we forgive you,"
said Winnie and Ginger.

Kissy promised never to get
them messy again. Then, they
all cuddled up together in their
basket and went fast asleep!

The End